Guide
to

The Non-Therapist
How to help
as if you were a pro

Kate
Tompkins
MEd RCT

with
significant
contributions from

Chaplain Christina Baxter MTS BCC

for
Coaches and Instructors

Guide to The Non-Therapist
© 2025 Kate Tompkins

Cover design: Rebekah Wetmore
Editor: Andrew Wetmore
ISBN: 978-1-998149-83-4
First edition April 2025
Moose House Publications
2475 Perotte Road Annapolis County, NS B0S 1A0
moosehousepress.com
info@moosehousepress.com

Moose House Publications recognizes the support of the Province of Nova Scotia. We are pleased to work in partnership with the Department of Communities, Culture and Heritage to develop and promote our cultural resources for all Nova Scotians.

NOVA SCOTIA
NOUVELLE-ÉCOSSE

We live and work in Mi'kma'ki, the ancestral and unceded territory of the Mi'kmaw People. This territory is covered by the "Treaties of Peace and Friendship" which Mi'kmaw and Wolastoqiyik (Maliseet) People first signed with the British Crown in 1725. The treaties did not deal with surrender of lands and resources but in fact recognized Mi'kmaq and Wolastoqiyik (Maliseet) title and established the rules for what was to be an ongoing relationship between nations. We are all Treaty people.

The Non-Therapist is a manual for
- ordinary people whom other people come to because they know they will listen.
- pros in their own field, trained ages ago; or whose main gig is not counselling, yet they find themselves counselling anyway.
- people who find themselves listening to other people's stories and thinking, "What on earth should I say?"

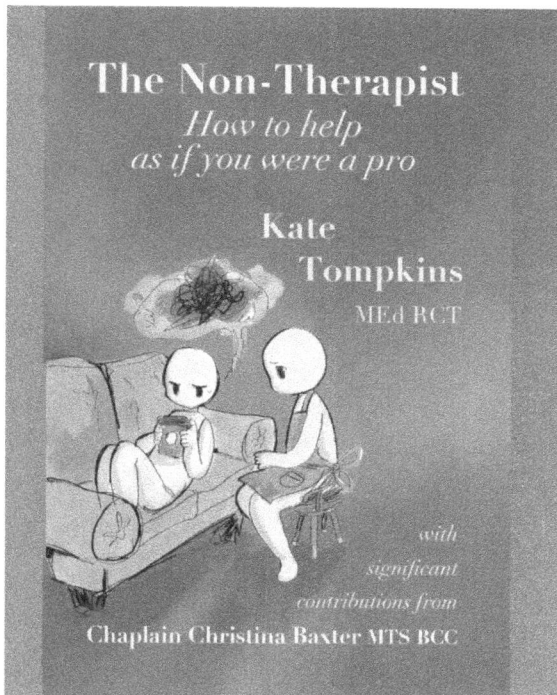

This guide will help you help those people get the most out of *The Non-Therapist*.

Dedicated to all the many people I have coached and taught over the years, and who are out there now, being awesome non-therapists.

Guide to *The Non-Therapist*

Introduction

Who is this guide for?

This guide is for anyone who wants to teach others how to help, using *The Non Therapist: How To Help As If You Were A Pro*[1].

You may be a college instructor who plans classroom exercises for your student community workers. You might be a support worker or coach meeting informally with a new foster parent in a comfy meeting room to discuss ways to improve their communication with a stressed child. You might be a granny who always has a pot of coffee on for visitors who wants to share helping strategies with like-minded community volunteer listeners.

I use the term "instructor" to refer to anyone wanting to pass on skills, either formally or informally.

The guide assumes that instructors have therapeutic listening skills under their belts but may not have a full range of adult education techniques and skills in their tool boxes. I'll provide both suggestions for activities best suited for classroom use, and activities for informal learning situations.

About 'The Non Therapist'

The Non Therapist is for anyone who wants to learn therapeutic listening skills. In particular, it is for these learners:

- Listening skills are (or should be) in their wheelhouse.

---

1   moosehousepress.com/product-page/the-non-therapist

- They will need therapeutic listening skills at a basic level for their careers or volunteer work, but they do not need a master's-level degree program in counselling skills.
- They want to change the world, one conversation at a time, by being involved members of their communities as helpers and listeners for friends, family, neighbours, patients, parishioners or clients.

What is in the book?

The Non-Therapist covers most skills that a beginner will need to be successful as a therapeutic listener. More experienced learners will also find resources and skills to add to their toolboxes to enhance their professionalism. Written at a Grade 9/10 reading level, it is accessible to most learners.

Throughout the book, I remind readers to clarify what their roles are (and are not), and when it is time to call in a pro. Understanding the limitations to their roles is essential.

These are the chapters:

1: What is this book about?
The opening chapter describes who the book is for, what readers will find in it, and explains terms and assumptions.

2: What on earth should we do?
This chapter helps readers to think through what their role will be, and what it will not be. For lay helpers, it also offers some thoughts about how to get started organizing a community peer counselling group.

3: Effective listening fundamentals.
This chapter builds the most important foundations for effective therapeutic listening, including empathy and compassion, authenticity, confidentiality, cultural contributions, and recognizing when it is time to call in the "big guns".

4: What on earth should I say?

Chapter 4 leads the reader through the seven key skills: listening well, interpreting body language, asking questions that draw out your client, being a mirror for your client, and clarifying, reframing and confronting in a helpful way.

5: What tools can I use with my clients?

This chapter includes helpful tools readers are welcome to swipe and use.

6: What should I expect?

This chapter outlines complaints that commonly walk through a helper's door, and offers guidelines for responding effectively. It covers depression, grief, anxiety, loneliness, emotional crisis, intimate partner violence, trauma and post-trauma, suicidal thoughts, self harm, substance abuse, sexual assault, child protection concerns, social justice issues, and situations in which multiple issues are involved.

7: Plan and structure a helping encounter

Not sure how to start? This chapter gives the reader a roadmap for what a helping encounter might look like and ideas for navigating the journey.

8: Wrap up

Useful articles, lists of resources, links, and suggestions for enhancing knowledge and skills complete the book.

Overall learning objectives

Here are the intended outcomes of *The Non Therapist.* Readers who complete the book will be able to:

- Reach people, draw them out, and help them explore their issues with easy-to-use listening techniques that can be helpful immediately; with tips on what ***not*** to do.
- Stop worrying about whether you might say the wrong words and make things worse.
- Feel confident that you know how to choose the best regional resources to refer someone who needs more help than you can give.
- Feel confident with user-friendly tools for supporting your loved ones, friends, colleagues, employees, neighbours, patients, parishioners or clients.
- Supervisors, HR people, and union reps can support an employee or colleague, resulting in satisfying work experiences and relationships.
- Professional helpers can gain or renew skills that complement and contribute to the other services you offer.
- Informal helpers can feel confident that they can assist their community by filling a service gap effectively.
- Incorporate your new skills into your current job or volunteer position.

Prerequisites

There are no knowledge or skill prerequisites for studying *The Non Therapist.* The content has been used to teach frontline mental and medical health providers, volunteers in community helping services, grannies who always welcome visitors who want to talk, clergy, hairdressers, cabbies, bartenders and many others. *The Non-Therapist* aims to develop a worldwide community of people who care and can use basic helping skills to support people who want to change their lives. Is this not how we make the world a kinder place?

The basic premise of *The Non-Therapist* is that anyone can be a useful human helper. Anyone can learn to listen well. It does not take a boatload of advanced training or fancy graduate degrees to be useful. It takes people with compassion, empathy, time, and a few key skills.

Instructing 'The Non-Therapist'

Teaching philosophy

The Non-Therapist makes these assumptions about the teaching and learning process:

- Anyone with at least a Grade 9 reading level can master the content.
- Those we help are capable of making their own decisions, managing their own lives, solving their own issues. Our role as helpers is to support that process, to assist our "clients" to create the circumstances in which they can change their lives on their own. If we attempt to do that for them, we rob them of the satisfaction and the learning that can happen when they do it themselves.
- Teaching may occur in a formal classroom setting, in a supervised practicum arrangement, or in 1:1 conversations and informal settings.
- The learning activities suggested are varied to respond to people's different learning styles. Some activities encourage "do-it-yourself" hands-on learning. Some activities are for personal reflection and writing. Some favour small-group or pairs exercises. Some people learn best from simulations and case studies. Role-play exercises cement new skills with hands-on practice.
- Instructors may choose from the suggested activities those that best match their students' learning styles and circum-

stances, the nature of the careers they are preparing for or the volunteer tasks they will engage in, the physical locales where teaching occurs, and the personal style and comfort of the instructor or coach.

- The learning objectives for your program should focus on demonstrated hands-on skills rather than recitations of knowledge without active "doing". I cannot see a leaner "understand" a concept, but I can see her explain the concept, or complete an action based on the concept.
- Assessing the success of teaching and learning is easier if we craft careful performance objectives based on feasible, observable, measurable action words. Objectives with "understand", "grasp", or similar words must be translated into action verbs such as "list" or "demonstrate" or "complete".
- The suggested approaches to assessing the success of learning are all action-oriented.

Recommended learning activities

Case Studies
Recommended for large groups in classrooms or small groups in less formal settings.

A case study is an example of a real-life situation presented orally, in writing, in films or in pictures. The learners practice dealing with the situation described in the case study by reviewing the example, identifying the issues, and planning solutions.

Case studies are an effective way to encourage group cohesiveness and group problem solving, especially in groups that are mixed in some way. Also useful for developing group cohesion and skills for working co-operatively. Encourages learning from one's peers and developing team support strategies.

Case studies are very useful for teaching a learner how to deal with problem situations without the risk of penalties for making mistakes in a real job task. The learner also can practice identifying important details and disregarding unimportant information.

Case studies can cover many different aspects of knowledge and skills that learners need to develop, and encourage them to think "outside the box" to analyze the scenarios provided.

Tips for success:

- Organize your small groups to represent a wide view of the world and to bring in different knowledge, skills and experiences. For example, representatives of different cultures, a mix of men and women of varying ages, from different types of backgrounds (for example, some big city types, some small towners). In groups of 4–6, learners can learn from each others' experiences and views of life.
- Case studies need to be well-prepared ahead of time. The scenarios must be realistic and in some way mirror what learners will deal with in their careers or volunteer assignments. Pose questions, describe problems, or decisions to be made that will prepare learners for real-life action.
- Timing is key. Present a case study for discussion **after** learners have been exposed to the knowledge and skills they will need to solve the problems posed. If asked to make decisions about topics before they have studied them, students will just become discouraged and may disengage from the learning process.
- Make sure that the scenario described in the case study contains all the information learners will need to address the questions posed. Don't be afraid to add in a few unnecessary details ("red herrings") so that learners will need to sift through them and select the most relevant details in the scenario.
- Follow up small-group discussions with some way to expand on what has been learned. For example, have each small group report back to the entire class about their discussions and conclusions.
- Case studies would generally be used as ungraded learning activities.

Role Plays

Recommended for either medium sized groups in classrooms, or for informal 1:1 learning.

Role plays cannot be beat for practising people-interaction skills, simulating a therapeutic encounter and practising specific listening skills such as open-ended questions, reflections of feeling, and the results of handing out unwanted advice, all in a safe way. Learners can practice real-life experiences without worrying about making mistakes in a real job situation affecting real people in need of help. Learners can also get an idea how other people feel, and what their concerns may be. Sometimes learners change their attitudes or behaviour after role playing and gaining deeper understanding of others' issues.

Tips for success:

- Prepare role play scenarios that allow learners to practice new skills in realistic narratives.
- Schedule a role-play exercise after the learners have had some time learning and practising the new skills. Role-play too soon, and the learners will be rehearsing how to do things incorrectly, and demonstrating those inappropriate techniques to others who are observing.
- Role playing is threatening to many people, since they are being observed and their performance analyzed. It is critical to build trust in the group first. There **must** be trust that any less-than-perfect demonstrations of skill in a role-play are treated as practice only, without any sanction for imperfections. The atmosphere must be one of intimacy, belonging, support and curiosity about experimenting.
- Many learners will refuse to engage in a role play if a person of authority such as a supervisor is present. Make sure there are no observing bosses, supervisors, managers or others in a position of authority over learners. Role-playing in front of people of authority is enough to send even the most confident folks into a tailspin. If the role play is a learning activity, admit no formal observers. If the role play

is an activity to assess the abilities of the learner before graduation from training, then including supervisors as observers makes a bit more sense, but it will still be stressful for the role players.

- In a large room with lots of people, set up two chairs for the role players in such a way that they have whatever privacy might be possible, without obstructing the view and hearing of the other learners. For more informal settings, set up the role play encounter in a private room with only the instructor and the role players present.

- List the learning objectives for the role-play exercise and how they relate to other job skills learned earlier. It is possible that each role player needs to learn a different skill.

- Set up the scenario to be role-played by giving each player a cue card (e.g. a 3"x5" file card) with all the information they need to play their role. Keep it as simple as possible. Address just one or two bits of knowledge or skills that learners will need to use. Complicating the story with "red herrings" will probably be a problem rather than a help in role playing. Discourage role players from showing others their cards or talking about their role before they do the scene, as there may be surprises or different information provided for each that would interfere with the scenario if shared.

- Help the players to relax. Assure them that whatever they act out will be acceptable. Give them a quiet corner to role-play in. Spend a moment to laugh or joke around before starting.

- Direct the players to identify their present feelings, then to imagine the thoughts and feelings of the characters they will portray.

- Other classmates are observers. Direct observers to look for specific things and not to interfere with the role players in any way (including no applause or cat-calls). For example, observers could watch for emotions expressed only with body language, or listen for things said that encourage cooperation.

- Do not interrupt role-playing unless the conversation dies or feelings get too strong.
- Stop the role play when it comes to a natural end, or when an important point has been made.
- Allow the role players to assess themselves before anyone else comments.
- Follow up a role play with sensitivity. In addition to asking probing questions (such as "What did you learn?" "What went well and what would you change?" "What steps would you take next?") be sure to also ask role players (in private, if there seems to be an emotional issue present) how they felt about the experience. Don't make role-playing a punishment that learners will choose to avoid in the future; make it fun, relaxed, light, and supportive.
- Then ask observers to describe what they saw and heard.
- Give learners feedback as to how well they performed the skills.
- Assign different roles to the learners so they can try out different styles or new ideas in a second role-play.
- Record how well learners demonstrated the required skills with a checklist, rating scale, or skills profile.

Pairs exercises
Ideal for informal 1:1 learning environments. But could also be used in a large group setting. For example, engage learners in a lecture by having them turn around to a neighbour to discuss a question or introduce themselves or express an opinion or practice a skill.

Also useful for mutual support when there is some potential risk involved, for instance, when doing street work.

Some examples of pairs exercises:

- Privately role-playing a therapeutic encounter to try out using open-ended questions, paraphrases, reflection of feel-

ings, or handing out unwanted advice.
- A field trip to meet and greet or interview a community resource agency.
- Researching some question or issue that can be broken into
parts or tasks for each learner to complete.

Tips for success:

- Ensure some form of privacy for the pairs, even if it is only a
"bubble" of space within a large group.
- If this is to be a graded exercise, make sure that everyone
involved knows ahead of time exactly how work will be assessed and graded. This can encourage a "lazy" partner to
do their share of joint work.
- Follow up on a pairs exercise by asking each individual to
describe their experience and what they learned. As a
teaching point, note how two individuals in the midst of the
same experience can have very different perceptions and
memories of the event. This can introduce a discussion of
individual differences and perceptions, where they come
from and what the impacts of those differences may be in
relation to the work or volunteer activity at hand.
- Pairs exercises will usually be ungraded learning activities.
If a pairs exercise is used as an assessment activity, both
members of the pair would be assigned the same grade.

Individual writing exercises
Recommended for informal supportive conversations or for homework for any learner.
    Individual exercises such as journalling and writing essays en-
courage learners to engage in self-reflection, and challenge one's
own assumptions and values as part of working out new ones. Also
a safe way to assess one's own knowledge and skills and plan for
future learning, without any personal exposure to fellow students.
Useful for reporting on information-gathering expeditions such as

checking out a new community resource.

Individual field research exercise activities are useful for developing initiative and independent thinking, gaining interviewing skills, enhancing 1:1 conversational skills and developing networks.

Examples include scoping out community resources, interviewing resource providers, analyzing one's own learning progress, locating information sources, and speculating about the future.

Tips for success:

- Remember that if the purpose of a writing exercise is quiet reflection, then the accuracy of spelling and grammar may be of much less importance. Keep the focus on private thought recording, and come up with some other way to assess academic writing skills if they are important to your learning plan.
- Make sure students understand the specific purpose for their writing, including any criteria to follow, to avoid someone going off on a tangent that is irrelevant to the intended learning at hand.
- If you are grading a private journal entry, then you will likely just check off the exercise as "completed." More formal pieces of writing, such as an essay, are generally graded by the value of the points made, and the inclusion of specific points the instructor is looking for. Grading writing can be very subjective, so a marking plan is needed to ensure that the instructor isn't handing out grades on the basis of which side of the bed she got up on that morning.

Simulations
Recommended for either classroom settings or informal settings.

Large group simulations help groups appreciate group dynamics and how they impact relationships. For example, a resource entitled "Ba Fa Ba Fa" is a classic group game that teaches what happens when two very different cultures encounter each other.

Simulations of a hands-on task are also useful for small groups or 1:1 learning. Simulations are simply a hands-on approximation of an actual task, but with no risks attached to incompletion or failure. Simulations can be completed as many times as needed until the learner gets the task 100% right. Provide feedback after each attempt and encourage more experimentation with the task.

Examples might include these suggestions:

- Role-play completing a complex form with a client.
- Complete a sample budget for a fictional project.
- Plan out the questions to be asked in an interview, and practice various ways of asking the questions so that they are comfortable and elicit the information you are seeking.
- Role-play the interview.
- Purchase role play games that already have the kinks ironed out of them.

Tips for success:

- State the learning objectives and explain how the simulation relates to skills learned earlier.
- Describe important or difficult points which the learner needs to pay attention to. Use a demonstration to draw a clear picture of what the learner is expected to do
- Make sure the task to be simulated is the same as is used in the field, up-to-date and accurate. We don't want to see rehearsals of an incorrect procedure.
- Use the correct forms, guidelines, procedures—everything as it will be in real life.
- For large group simulations, a great deal of preparation is required to make sure that the experiences the learners have in the simulation are actually teaching what you want them to learn. If an entire group learns the wrong thing, and reinforces each other's learning by engaging with others in the simulation, it could be disastrous.
- Give the learner directions and feedback on how well she is

doing. If the learner has difficulty with any step, stop and demonstrate the correct procedure, then allow the trainee to practice it before going on to the next step.
- After the learner has completed the simulation task, review the steps or procedures and give the learner feedback on how well he did. If the learner did not demonstrate the skills well enough, re-train, or allow more practice time before going on to a new skill.
- Simulations would usually be used as teaching activities. If a simulation were to be graded, it would be on the basis of accuracy, including all the required steps in order, and inclusion of all the relevant details.

Lectures
Lecturing has a long tradition in academia, especially for larger introductory level classes with many learners present. Unfortunately, lecturing has a lot of problems when it comes to successful learning. Few people are able to deliver a lecture that actually holds the audience's attention and results in them learning something useful. In more informal settings, lecturing can be a great way to lose your audience.

However, lecturing remains the fastest, most efficient way to transmit information uniformly to a lot of people at once, if the following pointers are followed:

- Find **any** way you can to stimulate more than one sense while learning.
- Include a hands-on demonstration, preferably one that listeners can practice right there in their seats.
- Encourage interaction with other people in the audience, for example a pairs exercise with the person sitting beside you.
- Add in an audio-visual resource for visual and auditory stimulation, and for learning through more than one sensory channel at a time. Don't expect the resource to do the

teaching, however.

- Hand around an object to be examined and commented on.
- Pose specific questions for which the audience can listen for answers. Include a handout with a "roadmap" where they can record the salient information as they hear it.
- Bring in a guest speaker to change up the energy for a few minutes.
- Invite members of the audience to contribute their thoughts to a topic from the floor, or bring them up to the podium.
- Hold small group workshops following the lecture in which learners can discuss the ideas presented in the lecture to deepen their understanding and think of ways to apply them to everyday practice.
- Mix lots of humour into your talk.

Lectures are solely a teaching activity; not used for assessment.

Demonstrations

Demonstration of a skill can be quite effective, since it uses more than one sense, which helps to cement the information in our brains. Demonstrations are perhaps the most useful approach for passing on a physical skill involving the hands.

Tips for success:

- Always demonstrate the **correct** way to do the skill. **Do not** demonstrate any inappropriate approach, because that is what learners will remember.
- Break the skill down into small steps and allow opportunities for learners to practice the skill themselves. Provide feedback and show them again if needed, followed by the learner trying it again.
- Arrange the room so that all learners can see the instructor's hands clearly. In a very large room, that may require cameras and screens for all to see the details.
- Have on hand enough pieces of material so that everyone in

the audience can try out the skill themselves, in the moment.
- Point out how the new skill is used and ask learners to speculate on using the skill in other circumstances or modifying the skill for some similar use.
- If a demonstration is used as an assessment activity, grade on the basis of accuracy in completing the task, following steps in order, and including all the relevant details.

Discussions
Can be used in any learning situation.

Large group, smaller group or even 1:1 discussions can be useful to develop a complex or novel idea using "group-think"; analyzing a situation or a resource from several different points of view and coming to a consensus on an important decision that impacts the group. Discussions can be used to help the learner understand a philosophical pillar of the organization, think about policies and procedures, or solve a problem.

Teaching discussions differ from ordinary, informal conversation in that there is a specific purpose to the conversation, something to be learned, and probably a list of questions to stimulate discussion. Conversation is usually open-ended and can go anywhere; discussions are planned and have specific beginning and end points. Debates are formalized discussions.

Examples might include:

- Debating the morality and impacts of choosing an action outside the expected norm.
- Debating a new policy or role a graduate might find themselves contending with at their workplace.
- Anticipating a future event in which the learner will need to use their new skills.
- Jointly planning a therapeutic encounter with a client, especially if the situation is unique or complex, or when it is not immediately clear what type of help is needed.

- Exchanging opinions about a resource's usefulness.

Tips for success:

- Facilitation of a discussion requires someone to be a moderator who will keep the discussion on track and manage the contributions of participants.
- A fruitful discussion needs some preparation. Have a list of questions for prompting ready. Open ended questions usually work well for stimulating discussion. The more provocative the questions, the more stimulating the discussion will be.
- Pay attention to body language and group dynamics. The moment you see signs of boredom or frustration, change gears somehow to keep the learners' attention. If you see signs of some other emotion, stop and ask the group if there is a problem they wish to raise or that you need to address.

Discussions are generally not graded.

Recommended types of assessment activities

The two basic rules for developing useful assessments are:

- Assessment must come directly from the performance objectives, which must contain action verbs.
- Assessment must be based on observable and measurable skills.

Written essay
Probably the least effective way to assess whether learning has been successful. Written tests mostly test the ability to read and write, rather than the ability to do the skill at hand.
   Useful for assessing learner's capacity to expand on or extrapol-

ate basic concepts to larger or new contexts. Also useful for assessing the learner's literacy skills. This is an intellectual exercise and does not show mastery of any hands-on skill, other than writing.

Grade on the basis of inclusion of specific points you are looking to find in the written product, not on spelling and grammar. Record the grade on a skills profile.

Multiple-choice tests, quizzes, exams
Multiple-choice questions mostly test the ability to remember, choose and discriminate knowledge intellectually. They are terrible at assessing active skills or creative ability. They have the advantage of taking little time or attention to score, especially with large class sizes. Since scoring is a simple yes/no comparison between the correct answer and the learner's choice, it can be done by an unskilled assistant.

For readers with good literacy skills, multiple-choice quizzes can be somewhat useful for assessing the learner's ability to choose between options, to identify useful as compared to extraneous information, and to identify patterns in data. However for learners whose first language is something other than English, and for learners with weak literacy skills, multiple-choice questions can be a disaster that cannot accurately assess their actual knowledge or skills.

Scoring is simple: each selection is either correct or incorrect.

Verbal explanations / demonstrations
Explanations are useful for describing the steps in an operation, but not for demonstrating the ability to actually do the task.

Add in a hands-on demonstration of the skills involved while explaining a step or a process to assess the ability to do the job.

Having the learner complete the task correctly, in a suitable time, in the appropriate circumstances is the only test of skill that actually assesses the learner's ability to do the skill accurately, and as needed on-the-job.

Document the demonstration of skills with a checklist, a rating scale, or a skills profile.

On-the-job observation

Useful for assessing how well the learner can take knowledge and skills into the actual workplace. Make sure that learners are aware ahead of time when and how they will be assessed.

Document the demonstration of on-the-job skills with a checklist, a rating scale, or a skills profile.

Assessment records

Simple Checklist

Useful for documenting information such as "did the learner accurately demonstrate the skill?" and "were all the steps followed in correct order"? A checklist is a simple "yes" or "no" record.

An example of a checklist:

Test Action	Yes	No
The student driver completed a three-point turn on a quiet road on the first try in less than 3 minutes.	✓	
The student driver changed a tire in the shop without help, and with appropriate torque, within 10 minutes.	✓	
The student driver changed a tire on the side of a moderately busy road, without assistance, within 15 minutes.		✓

Rating Scale

Rating scales are useful for documenting how well the learner did the task. More than a simple yes/no, a rating scale assigns a value to the performance. The value can be used as a pass/no pass guide.

For example, a rating of 1 or 2 would indicate where the learner needs to give more attention. A rating of 4 or 5 would indicate a "pass" grade. A learner could repeat a task several times until able to do it at the level required, at which point she has "mastered" the skill and it can be checked off as having been completed

An example of a rating scale:

5   I can do this very well, well enough to teach others

4   I can do this well, with no significant mistakes, without assistance

3   I am not sure, or neutral

2   I can do this, but only if someone helps me

1   I cannot do this at all

Test Action	Rating	Notes
Demonstrate smooth acceleration and deceleration between 0 and 50 KPH.	5 **4** 3 2 1	No significant issues; the deceleration could be more gradual.
Demonstrate successful parallel parking of a work vehicle on a busy street without assistance.	5 4 3 **2** 1	Misjudged the length of available space, dent in fender. Needs to practice choosing suitable parking space.
Demonstrate appropriate crossing of a level railway track.	**5** 4 3 2 1	Confidently completed all the steps in order. No issues.

Skills Profile

A skills profile presents the entirely of the knowledge and skills that a learner needs to master to be considered fully trained as a prepared and qualified practitioner of the career. The completed skills profile signals "graduation".

The profile breaks down job tasks into several "bands" of similar skills. Each skill has its own "box" where the instructor can record information such as a rating scale score, a yes/no completion, or date of completion.

Skills profiles have huge advantages for both the instructor and the learner. Seeing what he has accomplished so far and what he has yet to master can be very motivating for the student. For the instructor, there is a plan for developing training to help the learner master the required skills. When all of the boxes have been scored or checked off, then the learner can graduate from training and can take with him a record of accomplishment to hand to a new employer as proof of competency.

An example of a simple skills profile is on the next two pages.

Drive a Car Skills Profile

Demonstrate application of knowledge	Demonstrate correct application of rules of the road	Demonstrate correct response to road signs

Drive a company vehicle	Smoothly change gears in a standard-shift vehicle	Demonstrate smooth acceleration and deceleration between 0 and 50 KPH
	Smoothly merge with highway traffic from an on-ramp	Demonstrate safe braking on an icy road surface

Maintain vehicle	Change a tire on the side of a road	Check the vehicle's oil level and add the correct amount of oil to reach the correct level

Describe processes for obtaining a Class 4 license

Parallel park a work vehicle on a busy street

Demonstrate appropriate crossing of a level railway track

Choose safe speeds for the road conditions

Check the vehicle's tire pressure and add air to reach the recommended pressure level

Obviously, this example does not present a complete picture of a competent driver, but it illustrates how the various tasks required for assessment can be grouped and organized.

Add a box or two to a skill, and include a rating scale for the level of performance required, and you have a way to track the learner's progress over time. Check off each skill as it is correctly demonstrated at various levels. Or record the dates on which the learner demonstrated the skills.

Some skills profiles also add in what year of formal training (say, year 2 of an apprenticeship) the skills should be mastered. In this example, the final performance level required to illustrate mastery of the skill is level 3, and should be demonstrated by the end of year 2 of the training program.

Skill Level

3   Can perform this task satisfactorily without assistance and/or supervision.

2   Can perform this task satisfactorily but requires periodic supervision and/or assistance

1   Can perform this task, but not without constant supervision and some assistance.

0   Cannot perform this task satisfactorily for participation in a work environment.

The learner reached level 3 on June 1, as observed by instructor KT.

Parallel park a work vehicle on a busy street		Year 2
L3 ✓	L2 ✓	L1 ✓
June 1	May 12	May 1
KT	KT	BH

Notice that nary a "know" or "appreciate" or "understand" or "grasp" can be found on the skills profile; only action verbs. Translate all bits of knowledge that underscore behaviour into action verbs so you can measure them. I cannot see you "understand." I can only see you "do" something based on the knowledge.

Developing a skills profile that hits the mark is a lot of work and involves many people who know the job being profiled. A facilitator who is familiar with the process is very helpful. Contact the author if you want help developing a skills profile.

Additional resources

On the topic of assessment, these are golden oldies that set the standard for later writing:

- *Program Evaluation Kit*, Lynn Lyons Morris and Carol Taylor Fitz-Gibbon. Sage Publications,1978

  Evaluator's Handbook
  How To Deal With Goals and Objectives
  How To Design A Program Evaluation
  How To Measure Achievement
  How To Measure Program Implementation
  How To Measure Attitudes
  How To Calculate Statistics
  How To Present An Evaluation Report

- A series by Robert F. Mager. Fearon Pitman Publishers, 1973

  Measuring Instructional Intent (or Got A Match?),
  Preparing Instructional Objectives
  Goal Analysis
  Analyzing Performance Problems
  Developing Attitude Toward Learning
  Developing Vocational Instruction

For resources that informed *The Non-Therapist,* check out this site: seawinds-education.mykajabi.com/resources-for-the-non-therap-ist

Instructing Chapter One

Chapter 1, 'What is this book about?', sets the stage for the learner. It provides the rationale for saying that a helper does not need a boatload of fancy degrees, just compassion and a few key skills.

Key concepts

- Stats offer a glimpse into the reality of our situation: In North America, at least, our mental system is broken. For a variety of reasons, there simply are not enough trained professional therapists out there to help, if they are available at all.
- There is a gap crying out to be filled. Warm, compassionate people who are not professional therapists can fill it.
- There are a great many people who are already helping others without the benefit of a master's degree in counselling therapy or clinical psychology. Some basic skills, such as you find in *The Non Therapist*, will help them to be effective.
- "Help" is anything that contributes to someone coping with a human issue. Anyone can be helpful with compassion and a few key skills under their belt.
- Regardless of your job or volunteer title, if you find yourself helping but are not a professionally-trained therapist, you should find this book useful.

Chapter learning objectives

Learners will be able to:

- Quote recent stats describing the reality of mental health services in their own area.
- Describe why learning the skills of *The Non Therapist* will be helpful to their careers, volunteer tasks or personal lives.

Recommended activities and exercises

For classrooms

⇨ In small groups or pairs, have learners research the most recent stats that impact the need for counselling in their area. Have them identify possible sources of information to guide their research. Have them split up research contacts among the members of the group to encourage equal participation.
Materials: Phone book, phone, internet access
Time: 2 hours

⇨ Have small groups of learners debate the pros and cons of informal helpers using listening skills to help in their communities.
Time: 5 minutes for each side to make their case, 10 minutes for class to discuss and reach conclusions.

⇨ Ask small groups to create a list of topics or issues they can imagine they might need to deal with in their careers or volunteer activities.
Materials: flip chart and paper; markers
Time: 20 minutes to brainstorm, 5 minutes for each group to report to the class.

⇨ Ask learners to interview established helpers to learn what they do, where they do it, how they do it, and what they think is key for the learner to know.
Materials: notebook and pen; or digital tool
Time: 30 minutes each interview, over as many days or weeks as needed.

⇨ Have learners report on their research to their classmates. Facilitate a discussion about the most important points raised by learners.
Time: 5 minutes per small-group report, 20 minutes for class discussion.

For informal coaching

⇨ Have learners research the most recent stats that impact the need for counselling in their area. Have them identify possible sources of information to guide their research.
Materials: Phone book, phone, internet access
Time: 2 hours

⇨ Ask learners to interview established helpers to learn what they do, where they do it, how they do it, and what they think is key for the learner to know.
Materials: notebook and pen; or digital tool
Time: 30 minutes each interview, over as many days or weeks as needed.

⇨ Have learners journal their experiences and what they learned interviewing local helpers, and how they feel about learning and practising therapeutic listening skills themselves.
Materials: Personal journals and pens, or digital devices
Time: 20 minutes, or for homework

⇨ Ask learners to journal questions they have about their future,

using listening skills, and how they anticipate learning the answers to their questions.
Materials: Personal journals and pens, or digital devices
Time: Ongoing

Cautions

- There are no risky topics in this chapter.
- Some learners may want to skim or skip this chapter as being too academic. If the concepts are not key to the actual practice anticipated, going straight to the more meaty skills chapters would be okay.

Handouts

Questionnaires to guide and record research inquiries would be helpful.

Assessment

Assign "complete" or "incomplete" to journalling exercises.

Additional resources

Check out the resources for *The Non Therapist* here:
seawinds-education.mykajabi.com/resources-for-the-non-therapist

Instructing Chapter Two

Chapter Two, 'What shall we do?', is for those who want to establish a community-based helping service. It is also for helpers who already have a service but want to fine-tune its operations, and for government workers who support community non-profit organizations.

Key concepts

- Make sure your organization or group is clear on its mandate, and that individual staff and volunteers are clear on their roles and the type of help they will offer.
- Decide what expectations, assumptions, protocols and policies need to be developed, and how the organization will provide them to volunteers and staff.
- Make sure your service explores potential risks to the service, to the organization, and to staff and volunteers, and that it puts plans into place to reduce vulnerability and keep everyone safe.

Chapter learning objectives

Learners will be able to:

- Describe what the mandate of the group is and is not, what type of help will be offered, and what their own role will and won't be.
- Describe the organizational structure, policies and procedures that will best guide their service delivery.

- Make plans for the logistics of opening a new service.
- Express their own personal reasons for wanting to be involved in a helping service and assess how appropriate their choice is.
- Anticipate risks and dangers that may apply to their work and their service, and make plans to prevent problems and reduce risk.

Recommended activities and exercises

For classrooms

⇨ In pairs, research how other local services operate. Interview staff and volunteers of several different types of agencies to gather a spectrum of possibilities. Arrange to borrow or access their policy and protocol manuals and any other resources the agency can lend. Have pairs report back to the class.
Materials: Pens, research questionnaires
Time: 30 minutes per visit over days or weeks.
10 minutes per pair to report back to the group.

⇨ Have pairs or small groups design a fictitious service from top to bottom.
Materials: Flip chart and paper; markers
Time: 2 hours to design, 15 minutes for each pair or group to report progress to the large group.

⇨ Ask learners to journal their thoughts about their own desires to be helpers and assess their readiness to jump into a helping role.
Materials: Personal journals and pens, or a digital tool.
Time: 20 minutes, or for homework.

For informal coaching

⇨ Organize a brainstorming session with anyone who is involved (for example, staff, key volunteers, board of directors, local council, staff from other organizations your service might work in partnership with) to create your group's service guidelines.
Materials: Facilitator, flip chart and paper, markers.
Time: two hours.

⇨ Ask learners to journal their thoughts about their own desires to be helpers and assess their readiness to jump into a helping role.
Materials: personal journals and pens; or a digital tool.
Time: 20 minutes, or for homework.

Cautions

With luck, existing agencies will be welcoming and co-operative, and open to forming partnerships with a new service. However, it is possible that some might be protective and closed, fearing the loss of their own positions in the community, their funding sources, their physical space, or their staff and volunteers. Working together to solve local issues is not always the go-to response.

Handouts

Interview questionnaires.

Assessment

For the exercise in which learners design their own service, create a checklist of all the puzzle pieces that need to be in place for the service to be successful. As groups report back on their fictitious service, check off the inclusion of each item in their plan. Give the same grade to all learners in the small group.

Additional resources

Check out the resources for *The Non-Therapist* here: seawinds-education.mykajabi.com/resources-for-the-non-therapist

Instructing Chapter Three

Chapter Three, "Effective listening fundamentals", presents the most important foundations for effective therapeutic listening including empathy and compassion, authenticity, confidentiality, cultural contributions, and recognizing when it is time to call in the "big guns".

Key concepts

- Plain, ordinary empathy and compassion are essential tools for the helper.
- Being authentic is important, but not always easy, and there are limits. Authenticity for a helper is honesty, with discretion.
- It's not about you or what you may value. If you find yourself pushing, back off.
- The client is (usually) in control of the agenda, and that's okay.
- Don't blab! Don't blab to the client or about the client.
- Accept that sometimes there is very little we actually can do to be helpful, and adjust your Teflon cape.
- The client is their own best resource, and helping the client problem-solve is usually the most productive approach.
- Call in the big guns when you know you are out of your depth.
- Know the resources in your region you can refer a client to when more help is needed.
- You can quickly center yourself with a few simple techniques.

Chapter learning objectives

The learner will be able to:

- Demonstrate appropriate authenticity, empathy and compassion in role-play exercises.
- Describe and analyze the potential impacts of fundamental skills on helping encounters.
- In role-play exercises, identify when it is time to call in professional help and the most suitable local resource to refer the client to.
- Demonstrate two methods of rapid self-care.

Recommended activities and exercises

For classrooms

⇨ Foster an environment in which learners can explore their own issues safely, and encourage self reflection and pursuing professional help if needed.

As an instructor, it may not be appropriate for you to suggest that a learner seek professional therapy. It is important that anyone who wants to be a helper, in any capacity, has their own ducks in a row. If your learners' curriculum requires them to attend therapy, as many licensed professional programs do, then arranging professional time for learners is probably a task with your name on it. If attending therapy needs to remain a suggestion rather than a requirement, then do your homework. Identify approachable therapists in your area, learn what their specialties may be, how a learner can access their services, their costs and location. Assemble a binder of information for learners to consult privately.
Time: Ongoing

⇨ Demonstrate the successful use of the three self-care techniques at the end of Chapter Three. Ask learners to try them out as you demonstrate and to report on the subtle changes they observe.

Time: 10 minutes.

⇨ Have learners in small groups choose three fundamental concerns described in Chapter 3 for discussion. Ask the group to analyze the concerns by discussing these questions:

- What benefits does addressing this concern bring to a therapeutic relationship?
- What risks may be present if this concern is not respected or not practised appropriately?
- What steps should a helper take to ensure they are doing their best to address these fundamental concerns?

Time: 20 minutes to discuss in groups; 5 minutes to report back to the class.

⇨ Have small groups consider the case studies at the end of this chapter, or create your own. The closer a case study can come to what the learners will actually encounter in their jobs or volunteer activities, the more useful it will be as a learning tool.
Materials: Case study summaries
Time: 20 minutes to discuss each summary; 5 minutes per group to report back to the full group.

⇨ Invite a guest speaker to talk about their work, what is involved, what risks they have encountered and how they mitigated those risks, and how they measure success. Ask them to talk about the limitations they have encountered, and incidents in which they experienced "failure" with a client, and how they dealt with it. If the guest speaker is someone the learners may find themselves working with later, then networking can be a focus of the visit as well. Make sure there is informal social time for the guest speaker and the learners to mix and chat.
Time: 20 minutes for the presentation; 15 minutes Q&A, group chat, or meet-and-greet.

⇨ Based on their research of local services, have learners compile a reference binder. They could begin by developing a template that can be used to guide getting and compiling information consistently. Include the guidelines listed in Chapter 3 for researching helping services.
Materials: Binders, paper, and pens
Time: 2 hours

⇨ Role-play exercises. Facilitate role plays using the scenarios described at the end of this chapter.
Materials: Role-play cards
Time: 5-10 minutes for each exercise

For informal coaching

⇨ Foster an environment in which learners can explore their own issues safely and encourage self reflection and pursuing professional help if needed.

As an instructor, it may not be appropriate for you to suggest that a learner seek professional therapy. It is important that anyone who wants to be a helper, in any capacity, has their own ducks in a row. If your learners' curriculum requires them to attend therapy, as many licensed professional programs do, then arranging professional time for learners is probably a task with your name on it. If attending therapy needs to remain a suggestion rather than a requirement, then do your homework.

Identify approachable therapists in your area, learn what their specialties may be, how a learner can access their services, and their costs and location. Assemble a binder of information for learners to consult privately.
Time: Ongoing

⇨ Demonstrate the successful use of the three self-care techniques at the end of Chapter Three. Ask the learner to try them out as you

demonstrate and to report on the subtle changes they observe.
Time: 10 minutes

⇨ Together with the learner, identify which of the fundamental concerns your learner is already aware of and practising appropriately. Discuss specific examples in which the learner made use of or addressed the concerns.

Identify those fundamental concerns that the learner needs to brush up on. Analyze each of these by asking these questions:

- What benefits does addressing this concern bring to a therapeutic relationship?
- What risks may be present if this concern is not respected or not practised appropriately?
- What steps should a helper take to ensure they are doing their best to address these fundamental concerns?

⇨ Role-play exercises. Facilitate role plays using the scenarios described at the end of this chapter.
Materials: role-play cards
Time: 5-10 minutes per scenario.

⇨ Based on their research of local services, have the learner compile a reference binder. They could begin by developing a template that can be used to guide getting and compiling information consistently. Include the guidelines listed in Chapter 3 for researching helping services.
Materials: Binders, paper, and pens
Time: 2 hours

⇨ Visit a local resource service to talk about their work, what is involved, what risks they have encountered and how they mitigated those risks, how they measure success. Ask them to talk about the limitations they have encountered, and incidents in which they experienced "failure" with a client and how they dealt with it. If the service is one the learner may find themselves working with later, then networking can be a focus of the visit as well. Make sure there is informal social time for the learner to mix and chat with available staff.

Time: 1 hour

Cautions

As learners begin to adopt the communication style and skills suggested in *The Non-Therapist*, they may realize that their own personal style is worth fine tuning, or that their personal style needs to be significantly modified. While some students will accept this as being just one more learning goal to master, some may be thrown off-balance by the comparison between how they typically communicate and what is being asked for. Empathy, support and encouragement to attempt new techniques will go a long way to stabilize and soothe the upset learner.

Exploration of culture can be challenging. Everyone gets used to the tempo, sounds, accents, gestures, values, and expectations of their own culture and think of them as being the correct ones. "The way we do it is right". Which means that all others must be "wrong". It may require some exposure to new ideas before learners without a great deal of experience with other cultures can accept other ways of doing things as being just as valid.

Role-playing is a great activity for solidifying communication skills, but it is not for everybody. Those with "hands on", "group work" and "people interaction" styles of learning will thrive on role plays. But some people will be too anxious to actually learn from this type of activity, and could be traumatized by the attempt. Do not force role playing on any learner unless it is imperative that they be able to demonstrate certain skills. Try to find some other way to assess the skills if learners are extremely uncomfortable with role playing.

Handouts

- Role-play cards
- Case study summaries

Assessment

- Have learners verbally describe three fundamental issues they need to keep in mind. Have learners describe why the three issues they chose matter and how they might honour those issues.
- Create a checklist or rating scale, or use a skills profile, to monitor and record whenever you observe a learner effectively addressing fundamental issues in role play-exercises, in other activities or in ordinary conversation.

Additional resources

Check out the resources for *The Non-Therapist* here:
seawinds-education.mykajabi.com/resources-for-the-non-therapist

Case studies

Case Study 1

A woman comes to see you. She appears to be cowed and frightened. She has bruises on her face, neck, and arms, and is walking with a limp. Her response to your concerned questions is almost inaudible. She rarely makes eye contact, looks mostly at the floor.

A man has accompanied the woman. He is clearly very protective of her and jumps in to answer questions addressed to her. He tells you loudly that his sister wants help finding daycare for her children so she can go out to work. She bows her head, apparently in defeat.

When you attempt to get her alone without the influence of the man, he barges in and takes over the conversation. The woman does not say another word.

You give them information about local day care options and they leave, the woman three paces behind the man.

Discussion questions:

1. How do you read the situation?
   - What are the issues as stated?
   - What additional issues do you suspect or imagine?
   - What is the relationship between the man and the woman?

2. What fundamental issues do you need to keep in mind?

3. What is your role now? What action do you think you should take to help this woman?

Case Study 2

A man has wandered into your town, or your neighbourhood. He is dressed shabbily, and his hands and face are dirty. He is carrying an old, nasty-looking canvas bag. An emaciated dog is at his feet.

Some people walk by him, some pretend they don't see him, some stare with a hostile gaze. He makes his way to a soup kitchen, where you are a volunteer. Someone strikes up a conversation with the man, he starts telling stories of his exploits and horrors at war in the Middle East.

He asks you where he can find a place to sleep tonight. He mentions that he needs some privacy because he tends to have violent nightmares and he doesn't want to scare the others in a shelter. He looks like he needs a lot more than just a place to sleep.

Discussion questions:

1. How do you read the situation?
    - What are the issues you can see?
    - What additional issues do you suspect or imagine?
    - What are the man's immediate and long term needs?

2. What fundamental issues do you need to keep in mind to help this man?

3. What is your role now? What action do you think you should take?

Case Study 3

A mother brings her teenaged girl of 14 to your office. The girl clearly does not want to be there. She is wearing a top with sleeves that come about 2/3 the way down her arms. You think you can see some reddish scars on her arm just above the end of the sleeve.

When the mother leaves the room and the girl starts to open up, she talks about her despair because her boy friend dumped her. She talks about being bullied in school and that her boyfriend had been the only thing protecting her from the worst of the bullying. "Now", she says, "I don't know what I'm gonna do".

When you probe a bit, you learn that she is pregnant. She has not yet told her parents and she is afraid to, as she fears their reaction.

Discussion questions:

1. How do you read the situation?
   - What are the issues you can see?
   - What additional issues do you suspect or imagine?
   - What are the girl's immediate and long term needs? Which are the most pressing?

2. What fundamental issues do you need to keep in mind to help this girl?

3. What is your role now? What action do you think you should take?

Case Study 4

A neighbour child comes to play with your child. Normally, your child's friend is happy, bubbly, full of fun and energy. However, today she is quiet, withdrawn, close to tears. You notice bruises on her arm that looks like finger marks. She shies away from you when you try to hug her.

You have heard that there is financial trouble in the girl's home. It's just gossip, though; you have no direct knowledge of the family's circumstances. The girl is quiet for an hour or so of play, then she reluctantly leaves to head home.

Discussion questions

1. How do you read the situation?
   - What are the issues you can see?
   - What additional issues do you suspect or imagine?
   - What does the girl need from you?

2. What fundamental issues do you need to keep in mind to help this girl?

3. What is your role now? What action do you think you should take?

Role play scenarios

At this stage, the objectives of role-plays are:

- To expose the learner to life problem scenarios they may not have encountered in their real lives.
- To practice identifying and perhaps responding to the issues that were analyzed in the case studies.
- To practice keeping in mind the fundamental issues covered in Chapter 3 of *The Non-Therapist*.

It is too early in the training plan to be concerned about the learners demonstrating listening skills such as open-ended questions; that will come later. At this stage, any attempts to listen well should be applauded, even if they are not perfect, with the main focus of analysis after the role-play exercise being the fundamental issues.

Use the information below to create information cards for each character in each scenario. Give the appropriate card to each person who will be taking part. Collect the cards for reuse when the session is over.

Case Study 1 (three cards)

Woman:
You are in an arranged marriage that is not going as you hoped. Your husband is much older than you are and expects total control. Since your entire family emigrated together from the Middle East to this country, you have tried to loosen up the social ties that bind you to your husband, and he has countered by asserting even more control over you and declaring that he will not allow you to think like degenerate Western women. He thinks it is his right and oblig- ation to keep you in line, using any means he feels necessary.

Your brother, who has come with you to this appointment, sometimes is more protective than you would like, but you know he has your best interests at heart. Your husband does not want you to work, but your brother thinks it is okay in this country if you contribute to the family financially.

Man:
You and your entire family emigrated from the Middle East about a year ago. You are more liberal in your thinking than some of your family, and you think it's okay for women to have their own money and jobs. You believe in the importance of family and in maintain- ing some of the social traditions that you grew up with, although you are still struggling to figure out how those family values can be lived in this new society. You take your sister's welfare seriously and you are determined to see her succeed in this country.

You have come to this appointment today with your sister to speak for her and, of course, to protect her from prying eyes on the street.

Volunteer helper:
You are a volunteer with a drop-in agency that offers tax-return preparation help, financial counselling, and support and informa-

tion for entry-level investing. You are a student accountant and need these volunteer hours to fulfill a work experience requirement for your degree.

You have been warned that often clients bring personal issues into your information sessions, but, so far, this has not been much of a problem. Mostly people just want to talk about how to manage their money.

You care deeply about people and you are interested in their lives, although many of your colleagues are not. Your spirit is not as hidebound as some people who work with figures. You think of yourself as being more open to new experiences and ideas than many of your classmates are.

Case Study 2 (two cards)

Homeless man:

You are a veteran. You served in the Middle East for several tours of duty. In some ways, it was, of course, horrible to be in the middle of a war, but in other ways it was great. You made friends you will keep in your heart forever. You saw places you would never have seen otherwise. You were known in the local brothels and, off-duty, you had a pretty good time. It wasn't all bad, in spite of the death and destruction all around you.

Actually, it was pretty bad, when you sit quietly and think about those years.

When you left the service, you had a diagnosis of PTSD. You still have violent nightmares. Your mental health condition is precarious, at best. You have been living on the streets for a couple of years. You have not had a real home for some time. You do, however, have a beloved, affectionate pooch whom you feed when you can, though that is tough. Frequently, you share your meagre bits of food with him. The soup kitchens where you eat most of the time are pretty kind and don't mind if you take a little extra in your pockets for him.

You have made friends on the street, and try to stay away from the drugs, although you do enjoy a bit of whiskey when you can get your hands on some. Bathing is a problem, especially in the winter. In summer, you can wet yourself down in public fountains if you do it at night when no one is around.

In some ways, yes, life is tough, but in some ways it is pretty good. You like the freedoms that come with owning nothing and having no obligations. You have in the past resisted attempts from foolish know-nothing do-gooders who want you to conform to some standard they have in mind for you.

You have come to a soup kitchen for a meal. This particular kitchen is new to you. You are not sure where you and your dog will sleep tonight, but you are not too concerned about it. Something always turns up. You are more interested in avoiding the religious freaks outside the doors of the soup kitchen who are trying to waylay passing folks with their rhetoric.

Just as you step up to the counter to receive your meal, someone drops an empty kettle, which bounces around on the floor. The noise makes you jump a mile high—it is too much like being under fire, and you have a brief mini-freak out until your brain realizes it was only a pot. Not a bomb.

You know it was just your PTSD, so you shake it off and carry your food to a table.

Soup kitchen volunteer:

You are a middle-class parent whose kids are grown up enough that you can do some volunteer work to get out of the house twice a week. You don't really like the smells of some of the people who come here looking for food, but your heart goes out to them. You have never experienced poverty, homelessness, or real hunger before. Your life has been privileged and safe, for the most part.

A dirty, smelly man dressed in mismatched rags has just approached your serving station. He looks totally startled when someone drops a noisy kettle.

You have been briefed on the location of the local shelters, although you have never actually been inside one. This is one way you know you can help these poor people who seem like they are from a different planet.

Case Study 3 (three cards)

14-year old-girl:
Your mother has dragged you to see a counsellor, against your will.
You do **not** want to be here! You are pissed as hell at your mom for
doing this, although, deep inside, you know you need help.

You have been feeling more and more disconnected from your
friends and family over the past few months. You have started cutting again, after 18 months of not cutting. You are not even sure
why you do it, except that it feels good for a few moments.

School is the pits, with asshole gangs trying to corner you in
isolated places. Kevin, your guy, has been protecting you from the
worst of it. He's a big guy, likely headed for the armed forces. But
the jerk just dumped you for some hoe with bleached-blonde hair.

Just as you felt like maybe you could move on, guess what? Your
period was late. The jerk left you pregnant.

The world is dissolving around you. You are angry that you have
no control, angry at your mom, angry at school, angry at the boyfriend, angry at the world and, if you admit it, scared sxxxless.

Mother:
You are worried about your daughter. She seems a bit pale in the
face lately. You found a razor blade in her bedroom, and she has
fresh scars on her arms.

You have no idea what to do about that and you wish it would
just go away. It reminds you way too much of your own teenage
years, which were pretty disgusting. You don't know what to say to
begin talking to her, so you just avoid having that conversation.

But when you found a pregnancy test stick in the bathroom
garbage, you figured maybe you'd better take her to somebody.
Maybe she does not need to have the crappy life you had pregnant
with your daughter when you were just 15, and all that mess.

You are thinking about your new stud muffin, who has texted

you with suggestive comments, so you quietly leave the counsellor's office and sit in the waiting room so you can text him back without anyone seeing what you are doing.

Helper:
You are a worker in a women's resource centre. Your agency is known for its programs that support women from all walks of life with a wide range of issues. A woman has just brought her 14-year-old daughter in, but then the mom left the room without saying much.

The daughter's body language screams that she is angry, but you also sense something more that she is trying not to show. Her responses are monosyllabic, her head down. Her sleeve slips up and you can see fresh scars on her arms.

You are just starting a new job here, and you are anxious to do well. You are a bit nervous about this, your first case, as it looks rather challenging. But you care deeply and want to be useful.

Case Study 4 (two cards)

Child:
You are ten years old. Your mom and dad have been arguing loudly lately. You don't really understand what is wrong, but when you hear your parents fighting it scares you. Sometimes you hide in your room under the covers when they fight.

Last night was the worst. You heard your mom cry, and it sounded like your father hit her. She fell to the floor moaning and your father stormed into the next room.

You sneaked in to your mother and tried to help her stand up, but she was crying and holding her arm.

Just then your father came back in, grabbed you, tossed you onto the couch and yelled at you.

Your mom got up and put you to bed. Your dad left the house and did not come back before you fell asleep.

In the morning your dad came into your room and talked about going to Disneyland, for some reason.

Today, you are at your friend's house for a play date. You are supposed to go climb up into her tree house that her dad built for her, and read comics and eat junk food with her. You are sad and confused and you don't seem to have much energy, but you'd much rather be here than at home today.

Your arm hurts if anyone touches it, so you want to climb up into the tree house on your own.

Mother:
Your daughter's friend has come to your house to play, but she is not her usual self today. Normally she is talkative and funny, but today she is quiet and subdued, and she looks sad.

You go to help her up into the tree house where she and your daughter plan to have a girls' afternoon in, but she cries in pain and shies away from you. You notice bruises on her arm.

You are not close friends with the visiting girl's parents, but you know who they are. You know that the husband was recently let go, along with a lot of other people, when the plant closed.

Your daughter, who is already in the tree house, is calling to her friend to hurry up. You stand back and allow her to climb up on her own.

Guide to *The Non-Therapist*

Instructing Chapter Four

This chapter, "What on Earth should I say?", presents the key skills that will give your learners what they need to be as helpful as a pro.

Key concepts

- Listen with intention. Listening actively is the number 1 key skill.
- Show respect for your client's opinions, feelings, suggestions.
- Use attending skills to show acceptance, empathy and attention. Take what your client says seriously. It might matter a great deal more to your client than you realize.
- Do not avoid feelings or the "tough stuff".
- Learn what your client's involuntary and voluntary body language cues and vocal patterns communicate, and note ways in which they may differ from your own familiar patterns.
- If you must ask a question, use closed questions to gather essential information quickly and to limit conversation; use open-ended questions to build rapport and trust, to learn what is on your client's mind and to help her to explore deeper.
- Use specialized questions such as the miracle question and scaling questions to help your client explore further what could be in their lives.
- Don't be afraid of silence.
- Paraphrase content to gather and highlight facts, and use

reflection of feelings to explore emotional reactions. Focus mainly on emotions in a helping conversation.

- Listen for what is not said as a clue to essential concerns.
- Avoid giving advice or talking about yourself.
- Probe, summarize, reframe and confront supportively after a therapeutic relationship has been developed.
- To build trust and connection quickly, use a two-step approach: reflection of feeling followed by an open-ended question.

Chapter learning objectives

In role-play exercises, in learning activities, and in everyday conversation, the learner will be able to:

- Demonstrate active listening techniques.
- Demonstrate appropriate responses to clients' body language.
- Demonstrate the use of effective questions.
- Demonstrate the effective use of paraphrasing and reflecting emotions.
- Demonstrate effective summarizing, probing, reframing, supporting and confronting.

Recommended activities and exercises

For classrooms

⇨ Break class into pairs. Have learners take turns being the listener and the speaker (2 minutes of conversation for each, then switch roles; listener becomes the speaker, the speaker now listens.)

Topic: "How money and I get along"

The listener responds to everything the other says with a paraphrase.

Topic: "One thing I fear is..."
The listener responds to everything with a reflection of emotions.

Topic: "When I retire, I want...."
The listener responds to everything the speaker says with a closed question.

Topic: "One thing I value is..."
The listener responds to everything the speaker says with an open question.

Topic: "How I feel about my body..."
The listener responds to everything the speaker says with advice.

Debrief by leading a large group discussion with prompts such as:

- How did it feel to be the listener in each of these exercises?
- How did it feel to be the speaker in each of these exercises?
- Which techniques stalled the conversation?
- Which techniques facilitated the conversation?
- Which techniques would be most useful in each of the following circumstances:
    - The speaker is a frightened, child separated from parents in a busy airport.
    - The speaker is a survivor of a car accident that just happened.
    - The speaker is shy.
    - The speaker is angry.
    - You want to be helpful and acknowledge a speaker's words, but you are in a big hurry.

Time: 2 minutes for each pairs exchange then switch roles (about

20-25 minutes altogether)
For the debrief, about 15 minutes.

⇨ Ask learners to journal their thoughts about their own personal listening styles, noting what they do well now and what they want to spend more time learning or practising.
Time: 20 minutes, or as homework
Materials: Journals and pens; or digital tools

⇨ Ask learners to complete the "Exercises to Consolidate Learning" at the end of Chapter 4 of *The Non-Therapist*. Items 3 and 5 may have already been covered, if learners did the pairs exercises above. Have learners write their responses in their journals.
Time: 30 minutes, or as homework
Materials: Journals and pens; or digital tools

⇨ Obtain a copy of Bafa Bafa, a game that simulates the meeting of two very distinct cultural groups. A minimum of 24 people is needed to make this game work, but the top number can be very large. Consider inviting other classes to join yours. The directions for the game are fairly self-explanatory; however, to keep action flowing, it may be necessary to add in new elements to spark new interactions, especially with smaller groups. For example:

- "Oil has been found on lands protected by the Grandfather." Hand the grandfather a wad of "cash" from the trading culture to see what will happen.
- "Taxes are being raised on all incomes in Betaland. Grab some "cash" from some of the Betans and leave abruptly.
- A large group of Alphans visit Beta (or Betans visit Alpha), rather than just 1 or 2 people at a time, to spark more interaction and interest.

After the role play has come to an end (either naturally or because the clock is ticking), ask the Alphans to sit together on one side of the room and the Betans to sit together on the other side of the room. Facilitate a large group discussion with prompts such as these:

- Alphans, how would you describe the Betan culture? What did you learn about them from your interactions? (Conclusions will most likely be wildly incorrect and good for some laughs).
- Betans, set them straight. Describe your own culture.
- Betans, how would you describe the Alphan culture? What did you learn about them from your interactions? (Conclusions will most likely be wildly incorrect).
- Alphans, set them straight. Describe your own culture.
- Describe some of the comments you overheard during the game that represent prejudice, assumptions, fears based on lack of knowledge, insults based on differentness and so on.
- If examining culture or social dynamics is a part of your training plan, explain the concepts of integration, assimilation, domination, prejudice, discrimination, racism and culture shock, and ask which they saw happen in the game. (There is an infinite number of possibilities for the way the game evolves, there is no one right answer, no universal truth about what happens when two cultures meet.)
- Ask for a show of hands: "Who thinks they have been at any time the victim of prejudice?" "Who thinks they have ever been a perpetrator of prejudice?" Ask them to share their experiences, if they wish to. This question tends to elicit some emotional responses, so treat them sensitively. Many people will be surprised by what they hear, and may find their own assumptions or prejudices challenged.
- What is the most important thing you learned from this game?
- How will you incorporate that new thinking into your personal life, and into your career or volunteer activity?

Time: 2-3 hours for the game; 30-60 minutes for the group discussion.

Guide to *The Non-Therapist*

Materials: Bafa Bafa game
See note on p. 69

⇨ Facilitate role-play exercises. Use the same scenarios as in the previous chapter, or create your own scenarios. The objective this time is to effectively use the listening skills covered in Chapter 4 of *The Non-Therapist*.

Ask learners to observe what changes in the interactions when they use appropriate listening skills to respond. Ask them to compare the way this round of role playing evolved, as compared to the way the scenarios played out when they were practised in Chapter Three, and to speculate as to why that is the case. The focus is on the usefulness of these listening techniques.
Time: 10-15 minutes each
Materials: role-play cards (see p. 53)

For informal coaching

⇨ Pair your learner with a co-worker or a fellow learner. Have learners take turns being the listener and the speaker. (2 minutes of conversation for each, then switch roles; listener becomes the speaker, the speaker now listens.)

Topic: "How money and I get along"
The listener responds to everything the other says with a paraphrase.

Topic: "One thing I fear is…"
The listener responds to everything with a reflection of emotions.

Topic: "When I retire, I want…."
The listener responds to everything the speaker says with a closed question.

Topic: "One thing I value is..."
   The listener responds to everything the speaker says with an open question.

Topic: "How I feel about my body..."
   The listener responds to everything the speaker says with advice.

Debrief by leading a discussion with prompts such as these:

- How did it feel to be the listener in each of these exercises?
- How did it feel to be the speaker in each of these exercises?
- Which techniques stalled the conversation?
- Which techniques facilitated the conversation?
- Which techniques would be most useful in each of the fo -
  lowing circumstances:
    o The speaker is a frightened, child separated from par-
      ents in a busy airport.
    o The speaker is a survivor of a car accident that just
      happened.
    o The speaker is shy.
    o The speaker is angry.
    o You want to be helpful and acknowledge a speaker's words,
      but you are in a big hurry.

Time: 2 minutes for each pairs exchange, then switch roles. (about 20-25 minutes altogether)
For the debrief, about 15 minutes.

⇨ Ask learners to journal their thoughts about their own personal listening styles, noting what they do well now and what they want to spend more time learning or practising.
Time: 20 minutes, or as homework
Materials: pen and personal journal, or digital tool

⇨ Ask learners to complete the "Exercises to Consolidate Learning" at the end of Chapter 4 of *The Non-Therapist*. Items 3 and 5 may have already been covered, if learners did the pairs exercises above. Have learners write their responses in their journals.
Time: 30 minutes, or as homework
Materials: pen and personal journal, or digital tool

⇨ If you can assemble at least 24 people willing to take a few hours to have a fun learning experience, facilitate a game of Bafa Bafa as detailed on page 64.
Time: 2-3 hours for the game; 30-60 minutes for the group discussion.
Materials: Bafa Bafa game
See note on p. 69

⇨ Facilitate role-play exercises. Use the same scenarios as in the previous chapter, or create your own scenarios. The objective this time is to effectively use the listening skills covered in Chapter 4 of *The Non-Therapist*.

Ask learners to observe what changes in the interactions when they use appropriate listening skills to respond. Ask them to compare the way this round of role playing evolved, as compared to the way the scenarios played out when they were practised in Chapter Three and to speculate as to why that is the case. The focus is on the usefulness of these listening techniques.
Time: 10-15 minutes each
Materials: role-play cards (see p. 53)

Cautions

The same cautions as mentioned in the previous chapter about role playing need to be addressed.

Handouts

Info sheets about the nature of integration, assimilation, domination, prejudice, discrimination, racism and culture shock.

Assessment

For journalling exercises, a simple "Completed" or "Incomplete" is
all that needs to be recorded.

Prepare a checklist or rating scale, or use a skills profile listing
each of the listening skills you need to see learners demonstrate
for their careers or their volunteer work. Check off attainment or
mastery of a skill whenever you see it used in role playing, in other
activities or in ordinary conversation.

Additional resources

Check out the resources for *The Non-Therapist* here:
seawinds-education.mykajabi.com/resources-for-the-non-
therapist

Do an online search for "Bafa Bafa" and you will discover several
sources and additional resources for instructors.

A note about Bafa Bafa:
There really are an infinite number of possible outcomes to this
game (it's all about the relationships that develop and the group
dynamics). I have seen the following:

- The Aphans dominate the Betans.
- The Betans dominate the Alphans.
- The two groups decide to remain totally isolated from each
  other, never to connect again. Or one group does and the
  other attempts re-contact.
- Individuals, or sometimes an entire cultural group defect to
  the other culture.

- The Chief Betan Trader and the Alphan Grandfather get married to merge the two cultures. (The new version of the game may not have a grandfather).
- One culture falls apart for some reason and is assimilated by the other.
- Some individuals attempt to exist part-time in both cultures or take on characteristics of both to create a new hybrid culture.

Be prepared for noisy, spirited semi-chaos as you play the game, and even in the debrief afterwards.

Instructing Chapter Five

This chapter, "Freebies to swipe", includes helpful tools readers are welcome to take and use.

Key concepts

- Non-therapists can use these tools to help clients who are relatively stable and sane.
- Try out every tool first to become comfortable with it and be able to predict how clients will respond to it.
- Make sure you can demonstrate or model the skills and ideas yourself first.
- Adapt the tools as needed to be useful for your clients. If you are not sure how, please contact the author for advice.
- Make sure that you are relaxed, calm and focused yourself before using these tools. Make sure your Teflon cape is handy.
- If any issues arise, such as overwhelming emotions, troubling past memories, or anything else that seems unusual or out of place, refer your client to a pro therapist.
- Print out the triage tools as posters and place them where you can easily access them.

Chapter learning objectives

The learner will be able to effectively use at least one tool for exploring the past, one tool for exploring relationships, one tool for exploring mental health and awareness, and one tool for emotional self regulation.

Recommended activities and exercises

For classrooms

⇨ Ahead of time, have each learner prepare a summary of four tools from Chapter 5 of *The Non-Therapist*, one for exploring the past, one for exploring relationships, one for exploring mental health and awareness, and one for self regulation.
   Include the following information:

- Describe the tool. Note its purpose, its features and how it works.
- Discuss any cautions or additional information a helper needs to keep in mind when using the tool.

In the classroom, divide the learners into small groups. Have each learner demonstrate the appropriate use of one tool to the small group.
   Have the small groups vote on which tool they could see being the most useful in their careers or volunteer work. The learner who promoted that tool then gets to champion it to the large group.
   The learner's written or verbal summary of their four chosen tools can be graded.
Time: 10 minutes per tool demonstration, five minutes for voting, 15-20 minutes for large-group discussion.

⇨ If having the learners create their own tools is part of your learning plan, ask them to research and create any helping tool of their choice that they can visualize using in their careers or volunteer work. Then proceed as above.
Time: homework

For informal coaching:

⇨ Ahead of time, have the learner prepare a summary of four tools from Chapter 5 of *The Non-Therapist*, one for exploring the past, one for exploring relationships, one for exploring mental health and awareness, and one for self regulation. Include the following information:

- Describe the tool. Note its purpose, its features and how it works.
- Discuss any cautions or additional information a helper needs to keep in mind when using the tool.

Have the learner demonstrate the appropriate use of their four chosen tools to the instructor or co-workers.

Discuss how the learner can see using the tool in their work or volunteer tasks.

The learner's written or verbal summary of their four chosen tools can be graded.

Time: homework before the session; 45-60 minutes

Cautions

It is important that the instructor be skilled at using all of the tools in Chapter 5 before teaching this chapter.

Handouts

None

Assessment

Create a checklist or rating scale, or use a skills profile to assess learners' ability to use the four tools. The summary of the four chosen tools can be done either verbally or in writing.

Additional resources

Check out the resources for *The Non-Therapist* here:
seawinds-education.mykajabi.com/resources-for-the-non-therapist

Instructing Chapter Six

Chapter Six, "What should I expect?", outlines complaints that commonly walk through a helper's door, and offers guidelines for responding effectively. We cover depression, grief, anxiety, loneliness, emotional crisis, intimate partner violence, trauma and posttrauma, suicidal thoughts, self harm, substance abuse, sexual assault, child protection concerns, social justice issues, and people with multiple issues.

Key concepts

- Listening well is the recommended first step in any situation in which a helper is engaged.
- Looking after practical matters is a key role for a helper.
- Don't be afraid to take whatever action is required to support your client, friend, or community.

Chapter learning objectives

Learners will be able to:

- Describe appropriate ways to respond to all of the main topics detailed in chapter six of *The Non-Therapist*
- Respond appropriately to at least three of those issues when they encounter them in role-play exercises.

Recommended activities and exercises

For classrooms

⇨ Invite a series of expert guest speakers from local non-profit groups, agencies and organizations providing support for people experiencing the issues detailed in chapter six of *The Non-Therapist.* Talking points might include these:

- Whom does your service support?
- How does your service support your clients?
- What are the main issues you see?
- What challenges or obstacles do you encounter when trying to help people?
- What should the general public know about what you do?
- What should helpers know about what you do or about your clients and their issues, beyond the basics?

Time: Allow for a 20 minute meet and greet, Q&A or informal social-izing afterwards so learners can mix with the guest speakers.

⇨ In small groups, revisit the case studies in "Instructing Chapter Three" (or create new case studies that mirror the circumstances learners will be working in after graduation) with these discussion questions:
- Referring to the learners' future career or volunteer work, what is the role of a helper in this scenario? What is it NOT?
- What is the best way for a helper to respond to this scenario?
- What potential risks are likely to accompany engaging with the people in this scenario?
- At what point in this scenario should a helper call in a pro?

Materials: Case study descriptions and discussion questions
Time: 20 minutes for discussion in small groups.

⇨ Role play. Ask learners to generate several role play scenarios based on the issues detailed in chapter six of *The Non-Therapist*. Have learners role-playing the helper respond using all of the skills learned to date.
Materials: role-play cards
Time: 10-15 minutes for each scenario

⇨ Arrange for learners to shadow experienced workers to network, observe and learn about the issues and how to respond to them, and gain familiarity and confidence with the issues and the services. For example:

- Accompany a crisis intervention worker on a call.
- Listen in on a crisis intervention phone call.
- Attend workshops, seminars, public meetings of local agencies and organizations to network and learn about the issues.
- Observe a counselling session, unobtrusively.
- Volunteer to work in a hospital, nursing home or halfway house to provide emotional support services.
- Accompany a social worker, family support worker or similar pro on home visits.
- Sit in on court cases involving domestic issues, if the public is allowed entry.
- Volunteer to work at local nonprofits and agencies such as a food bank, telephone crisis centre, women's support centre, rape crisis centre, homeless shelter, or a soup kitchen.

Consider assigning shadowing gigs in pairs, for mutual support, to learn from each other, and to increase personal safety for the helper.
  Debrief by asking the learners what they learned from their job shadowing experience.
Time: as much as is needed.

⇨ Subscribe to magazines aimed at career members of the profes-

sion, and make them easily available to learners to read informally when time allows.
Materials: magazines
Time: ongoing

⇨ Screen movies or educational documentaries that deal with the issues learners will engage with after graduation.
Materials: Movies, suitable technology to play them
Time: ongoing

For informal coaching

⇨ Arrange for the learner to visit local non-profit groups, agencies and organizations providing support for people experiencing the issues detailed in chapter six of *The Non-Therapist*. Talking points might include:

- Whom does your service support?
- How does your service support your clients?
- What are the main issues you see?
- What challenges or obstacles do you encounter trying to help people?
- What should the general public know about what you do?
- What should helpers know about what you do or about your clients and their issues, beyond the basics?

Time: 30 minutes each, over as many days or weeks as needed.

⇨ Revisit the case studies in "Instructing Chapter Three" (or create new case studies that mirror the circumstances the learners will be working in after graduation) with these new discussion questions:

- Referring to the learner's future career or volunteer work, what is the role of a helper in this scenario? What is it NOT?

- What is the best way for a helper to respond to this scenario?
- What potential risks are likely to accompany engaging with the people in this scenario?
- At what point in this scenario should a helper call in a pro?

Materials: case study descriptions and discussion questions
Time: 10-15 minutes per case study

⇨ Role play. Ask learner to generate a few role-play scenarios based on the issues detailed in chapter six of *The Non-Therapist*. Have the learner role play the helper in the scenario, using all of the skills learned to date.
Materials: role play cards
Time: 10-15 minutes each

Arrange for learner to shadow experienced workers to network, observe and learn about the issues and how to respond to them, and gain familiarity and confidence with the issues and the services. For example:

- Accompany a crisis intervention worker on a call
- Listen in on a crisis intervention phone call.
- Attend workshops, seminars, public meetings of local agencies and organizations to network and learn about the issues.
- Observe a counselling session, unobtrusively.
- Volunteer to work in a hospital, nursing home or halfway house to provide emotional support services.
- Accompany a social worker, family support worker or similar pro on home visits.
- Sit in on court cases involving domestic issues, if the public is allowed entry.
- Volunteer to work at local nonprofits and agencies such as a food bank, telephone crisis centre, women's support centre, rape crisis centre, homeless shelter, or soup kitchen.

Debrief by asking the learner what they learned from their job shadowing experience.
Time: as much as is needed.

⇨ Subscribe to magazines aimed at career members of the profession, and make them easily available to the learner to read informally when time allows.
Materials; magazines
Time: ongoing

⇨ Screen movies or educational documentaries that deal with the issues the learner will engage with after graduation.
Materials: Movies, suitable technology to play them
Time: Ongoing

Cautions

Once learners begin to volunteer, shadow or work in a helping situation, their own emotional baggage will emerge. It is important that learners have done whatever is needed to be able to engage with those needing help without triggering their own memories and emotions.

Be prepared to support in any way and debrief after a helping encounter so that learners can vent as they need to clear their own stuff out of the way. It is very common, and very upsetting, for a learner to find themselves dealing with some big emotions after a challenging call, say a suicide.

Handouts

Role play cards, case study summaries.

Assessment

Prepare a checklist or rating scale, or use a skills profile, to record the learners' achievement of this chapter's objectives while job shadowing and role playing.

Additional resources

Check out the resources for *The Non-Therapist* here: seawinds-education.mykajabi.com/resources-for-the-non-therapist

Instructing Chapter Seven

Chapter Seven, "Plan and structure a helping encounter", gives the reader a roadmap for what a helping encounter might look like and ideas for navigating the journey.

Key concepts

- Plan a helping encounter when you can, and just dive in when helping is spontaneous.
- Be flexible and open to the unexpected.

Chapter learning objectives

Describe the four stages of an ideal therapeutic interview, and demonstrate moving through them in role play exercises.

Recommended activities and exercises

For classroom and informal coaching

⇨ Ask learners to brainstorm open-ended questions that could be used as prompts in each of the four stages of an ideal therapeutic interview.
Materials: Flip chart paper, marker pens
Time: 15 minutes

⇨ Ask learners to create role play scenarios based on their future work. Learners playing the helper in the role play will use all of the skills learned to date.

Have observers watch for specific things, for example:

- Did the helper move through all stages appropriately?
- What helpful techniques did you notice in each stage?
- What was the impact of those techniques on the person with the issue?

Have role players answer these questions:

- How did it feel to be the person with the issue in this role play?
- How did it feel to be the helper?
- Helper, what did you do that helped?
- Helper, what would you like to improve on?

Time: 20-30 minutes per role-play and feedback

Cautions

Consider the usual cautions re role playing.

Handouts

None.

Assessment

Create a checklist or rating scale, or use a skills profile, to note mastery of the objectives in this chapter, and the skills learned in other chapters. By this point, learners should be able to demonstrate mastery of all skills taught in *The Non-Therapist*. The completed skills profile or the collection of checklists and rating scales signals completion of training.

for Instructors and Coaches

Additional resources

Check out the resources for *The Non-Therapist* here:
seawinds-education.mykajabi.com/resources-for-the-non-therapist

Instructing Chapter Eight

Chapter Eight wraps up *The Non-Therapist*. Useful articles, lists of resources, links, and suggestions for enhancing knowledge and skills complete the book.

Key concepts

- Learning can be a life-long adventure. An effective helper is always on the lookout for new ideas, new research, new tools, and new skills to add to their toolbox.
- Focus your research on trusted websites.

Chapter learning objectives

Learners will be able to:

- Assess their own skills.
- Describe at least three ways to learn more.

Recommended activities and exercises

For classroom and informal coaching.

⇨ Have learners complete the self assessment quiz in Chapter Eight of *The Non-Therapist*. Pair learners off to discuss their self assessment and their plans for further learning.
Time required: 15 minutes

⇨ Have learners journal their thoughts about their learning program, their new skills and their future plans.
Time required: 20 minutes, or as homework

Cautions

Make sure learners can explain the concept that not all websites are equal, and that research should focus on reliable respected sites.

Handouts

List of recommended resources for further learning.

Assessment

No assessment is required of this chapter's learning. Assessment at this point is of the entire program and the sum total of all skills learned in training.

If the learner's self assessment is different from the instructor's assessment records, then some discussion with the learner is required to determine the reasons for any discrepancies and what action should be taken.

Additional resources

Check out the resources for *The Non-Therapist* here:
seawinds-education.mykajabi.com/resources-for-the-non-therapist

Glossary

This glossary covers terms in both *The Non-Therapist: How To Help As If You Were A Pro* and *Guide To The Non-Therapist*.

Audio-visual resource: Any teaching aid that uses sound, images, or both to engage learners.

Authenticity: The degree to which a person's actions are congruent with their beliefs and desires. Being true to one's own personality, spirit, or character. Authenticity for a helper is honesty, with discretion. It's openness, without sharing stuff that will make the client feel uncomfortable or damage the therapeutic nature of the relationship.

Bafa Bafa: A role-play game that simulates encounters between two very different cultures, Alpha and Beta, to observe group interaction and how cultures evolve.

Boundaries: Setting boundaries is a way of teaching those we are involved with about how we want to be treated.

Case Study: An example of a real-life situation presented orally, in writing, in films or with pictures. Learners practice dealing with the situation described in the case study by reviewing the example, identifying the issues, and proposing solutions.

CBT: Cognitive behavioural therapy is the gold-standard treatment for mild to moderate depression, anxiety and many other issues. CBT is one of the most extensively-researched techniques in psychotherapy. The basic premise is that our thoughts create our emotions, and that we can turn around many unwanted emotional states by learning to think differently about life.

Client: Anyone a helper helps.

Closed questions: A question that requires only a simple yes or no response, or a factual response ("What is your name?"). Good for gathering details quickly, as in an emergency. Used also to limit and express control over the conversation

Compassion: Both an understanding of another's pain and the desire to somehow mitigate that pain. Compassion feeds the motivation to learn how to be helpful.

Confidentiality: In helping, we express confidentiality by ensuring that all records are kept securely; by keeping secret all client information; by not discussing clients with anyone else for any reason, without their express permission.

Dependency: A client is so relieved that someone is listening, that they relax so much that they would rather hand their problem over to the counsellor to solve rather than taking steps themselves. They become dependent on the helper.

Discussion: An intentional conversation facilitated by an instructor. Discussions differ from ordinary, informal conversation in that there is a specific purpose to the conversation, something to be learned, and probably a list of questions to stimulate discussion.

Empathy: The ability to imagine or understand how someone might feel, without necessarily having those feelings yourself. "Showing empathy" means being able to get right under your client's skin and see the world from their point of view, then letting them know that you have seen and understood.

Help: Anything that contributes to someone coping with a human issue. Anyone can be helpful with compassion and a few key skills under their belt.

Helper: Compassionate individual, whether paid or volunteer, trained or amateur, who chooses to be of assistance to others. Includes informal helpers, lay or peer counsellors, supportive listeners, frontline workers, paraprofessionals, and professionals in helping professions. Any volunteer or salaried person who is not a professionally-trained therapist but is helping others anyway, using listening skills and therapeutic tools and techniques.

Incongruity: The body language says one thing and the words say another.

Inconsistency: The details of a story are told one way today and another way tomorrow.

Instructor: Anyone who wants to pass on skills, either formally or informally. Includes 1:1 coaching as well as classroom teaching.

Learning objective, performance objective: The final performance objective is a statement of exactly what skills the learner needs to be able to demonstrate in order to prove mastery of the skill. Learning objectives may be successive steps leading to the final performance objective.

Miracle questions: Questions that create the thought that, overnight, a miracle has happened. Use the miracle question to encourage a client to think about what could be, and to take steps towards creating the desired situation. "What if, overnight while you were sleeping, a miracle happened? You wake up, and your relationship is suddenly a 10 out of 10. It's fantastic. What would that look like? What would it feel like?"

Open-ended questions: Questions that require more than a yes or no response, and are wide open to allow the speaker to respond in any way they wish. They encourage the speaker to say more by giving her the power to choose what to say or not say.

Paraphrasing: Repeating back to the client what has been said, but in one's own words, and in a way that demonstrates that the listener has taken in what the client has said, and that encourages more sharing. Paraphrasing focuses on facts and details.

Pro: A professional helper who has been trained to help others. For example, psychologists, clinical social workers, addictions counsellors, police officers, physicians.

Probing: A combination of paraphrasing and asking questions. Probes are designed to obtain information from another person. Since probing can backfire, use it sparingly, gently, and respectfully.

Pseudo-questions: These are not really requests for information at all. They are, in fact, a passive-aggressive attack, a way for the questioner to try to gain some advantage over the other person.

PTSD: Post Traumatic Stress Disorder is a condition in which the nervous system and brain get hijacked by an old memory and the emotions associated with it. The symptoms may include a number of rather distressing emotions and behaviours that can trouble the client significantly and that feel out of the client's control to change.

Rating scale: A way to assess how well a learner performed a task. Includes a description of various level of performance.

Reflection of feeling: Reflecting emotions is very similar to paraphrasing, except the focus is not on facts and details but on feelings and perceptions. It is like holding up a mirror so that the speaker can see herself more clearly.

Reframing: Helping the client see and think differently about their situation. It's all about planting the seeds of possibility.

Role playing: A learning activity in which learners act out roles in a scenario in order to practice using new skills without worrying about making mistakes, or to learn about conditions and issues they may encounter in real life.

Scaling question: This tool asks a client to rate on a scale of 0 -10, or 0 – 100, what level an emotion might be at this particular moment, or how much the client actually believes some thought. Scaling questions imply that an emotional sensation can change over time, and that the client may be able to do something to manage that emotion. It might also imply that a thought, for example a negative impression of oneself, might also be changeable.

Self-harm: Usually refers to a person purposely cutting themselves as a response to the pressures in their lives.

Simulation: A learning activity that mimics an actual task, for the purpose of learning without worrying about making mistakes in real life.

Skills Profile: A document that lays out the entire scope of a job or profession. Individual skills are arranged in like groups to organize the learner's knowledge and skills into bite-sized pieces. Additional information can be added to document and score the learner's progress.

Social justice: The idea that all people should have equal access to wealth, health, well-being, justice, privileges, and opportunity, regardless of their legal, political, economic, or other circumstances; and that governments, organizations and individuals have a moral responsibility to redress any circumstances that do not respect and promote this premise. Equality, equity, rights, and participation are some of the principles of social justice.

Sociogram: A drawing depicting a client's relationships with family, friends, and community.

Supportive confrontation: Supportive confrontation is the art of challenging the client while still ensuring your support. One of the simplest ways to confront helpfully is to point out inconsistencies and discrepancies. Humour can help with that task.

Therapeutic encounter: A meeting of a helper and a client that is intended to provide support or assistance, especially about a personal or emotional issue. May be spontaneous or planned.

Therapeutic listening skills: Techniques the helper deploys to listen for the purpose of offering assistance to someone else. They differ from ordinary conversational skills in that they are intentional, and the helper is attempting to engage the client emotionally in order to explore the speaker's thoughts and emotions with a view towards problem-solving. Includes skills such as open-ended questions, reflection of feelings, paraphrasing, probing, clarifying, and confronting.

Transference: The client transfers to the helper the affection and love that they should be giving to a partner or other family member.

VPTSD: Vicarious Post Traumatic Stress Disorder. VPTSD results after a helper hears details of a client's traumatic experiences.

About the author

Kate Tompkins is a rather white-haired curmudgeon whc has been around the block several times. In her 50 years as a therapist and adult educator, she has worked with many small communities in crisis, and helped create community support groups, peer counselling groups, local shelters and crisis support phone lines. She has taught counselling skills to frontline workers, such as nurses, social workers, addictions counsellors, supervisors and union reps; and runs on-line in-service courses for therapists.

Kate is currently a Registered Counselling Therapist with a private practice in Nova Scotia, Canada; and an adult educator. She lives in a sleepy town with her two dogs, a sailboat and a penchant for musical theatre.

Photo by Brian Collins, Landwash Studios